Pebble® Plus

Fun STEM Challenges

BUILDING SUNSHADES

by Marne Ventura

PEBBLE
a capstone imprint

Pebble Plus is published by Pebble, an imprint of Capstone.
1710 Roe Crest Drive, North Mankato, Minnesota 56003
www.capstonepub.com

Library of Congress Cataloging-in-Publication data is available on the Library of Congress website.
ISBN: 978-1-9771-1301-6 (library binding)
ISBN: 978-1-9771-1781-6 (paperback)
ISBN: 978-1-9771-1307-8 (ebook pdf)

Summary: Describes uses for sunshades and how to make and test them.

Image Credits
Photographs by Capstone: Karon Dubke;
Marcy Morin and Sarah Schuette, project production;
Heidi Thompson, art director

Shutterstock: Air Images, 7, CGN089, 1, Chiyacat, 5

All the rest of the images are credited to: Capstone Studio/Karon Dubke

Editorial Credits
Erika L. Shores, editor; Juliette Peters, designer;
Eric Gohl, media researcher;
Laura Manthe, production specialist

All internet sites appearing in back matter were available and accurate when this book was sent to press.

Capstone thanks Darsa Donelan, Ph.D., assistant professor of physics, Gustavus Adolphus College, St. Peter, MN, for her expertise in reviewing this book.

Printed in China.
2493

Table of Contents

What Is a Sunshade?

Sunshades are all around you. Umbrellas, trees, and tents are sunshades. Hats and caps are too.

Why Build Sunshades?

The sun sends out heat and light. Sunshades block heat and light. Sunshades keep you cool. They keep you from getting a sunburn.

Make Your Own

Gather white and black paper, straws, plastic lids, and clay. Find ice cubes and small plastic bags that zip too. What else can you use to make a sunshade?

Make a sunshade that looks
like an umbrella. Make one
that looks like a tent. Do both
shapes make shade? Which shape
would you rather use at the beach?

Make a tent with black paper.

Use white paper to make another tent.

Place your tents in the sun.

Which tent feels warmer inside?

Do you know why?

13

Make the top of one umbrella
tilt away from the sun.
Make another one tilt toward
the sun. Which one blocks
more heat and light?

toward the sun

away from sun

This umbrella was put on
the sidewalk in the morning.
As the sun moves, the shadow
moves, too. Where will its shadow
be in the afternoon?

Put an ice cube into each small bag.
Put them in the sun. Cover one with
your sunshade. Which ice cube
melts first? Repeat using sunshades
in other shapes and colors.

What Did You Learn?

Sunshades can have open
or closed sides. They block
the sun's light. The shadow made
by a sunshade moves with the sun.

Glossary

angle—how much something is slanted or sloped

block—to stop

heat—being warm or hot

light—brightness that lets us see, such as rays from the sun

shade—darkness and coolness caused by blocking sunlight

shadow—shade made by something that blocks light

tent—a type of sunshade used for shelter

tilt—the slant or angle of something

umbrella—a type of sunshade on a pole

Read More

Boothroyd, Jennifer. *What Does Sunlight Do?* Minneapolis: Lerner Publications Company, 2015.

Dunne, Abbie. *Light.* North Mankato, MN: Capstone, 2017.

Lindeen, Mary. *Sun and Shade.* Chicago: Norwood House, 2018.

Internet Sites

Light for Kids
http://www.sciencekids.co.nz/light.html

What Is a Shadow?
http://kinooze.com/what-is-a-shadow/

Critical Thinking Questions

1. What different kinds of sunshades have you used before?

2. How can you make a sunshade with paper?

3. How do sunshades help people?

Index